21st Century Sonship

Restoring the Art of

Apprenticeship

21st Century Sonship:
Restoring the Art of Apprenticeship

Jonathan G. Pitts

Published by Greater Works Publishing
A Division of Greater Works Enterprises, LLC
www.greaterworksenterprises.com
2016

First Printing: 2016

ISBN 978-0-9975643-3-4

Greater Works Publishing
A Division of Greater Works Enterprises, LLC
Website: www.greaterworksenterprises.com

Scripture quotations taken from the Holy Bible, King James Version, Cambridge, 1769.

Scripture taken from the Amplified Bible, Copyright © 1954, 1958, 1962, 1964, 1965, 1987 by The Lockman Foundation. Used by permission.

Dedication

To the sons (both spiritual and natural) who desire to honor the Father by serving their fathers.

To the Pastors and Leaders raising sons and investing in the next generation for the glory of the Lord.

This book is dedicated to you – God bless you for all that you do.

<u>Also Available By Jonathan G. Pitts</u>

Heaven's Sound: Call to the Nations

Ministering to Millennials: The Challenges of
Reaching Generation "Why"

<u>Connect with Jonathan</u>

Facebook: Jonathan Pitts
Twitter: @JonathanGPitts
Instagram: Jonathan_G_Pitts

Table of Contents

INTRODUCTION

S onship – What do you think about when you hear this word? Initially, most people may think of the obvious relationship of a male child to a parent. Perhaps they may even consider additional points such as whether the child takes on certain attributes or influences from the parents and consider the evidence of these in the child's life as sonship. Those who may have been around church settings for any length of time may have heard the word spoken every now and then in relation to a person and his/her relationship with the Pastor or another ministry figure. Biblically, it is mentioned in various forms whether by Jesus acknowledging his Father in Heaven or the Creator saying Jesus is His Son in whom He is well pleased. Paul speaks of Timothy and Titus as "sons" (1 Timothy 1:2; Titus 1:4) in relation to the fact of his training them in ministerial capacities, planting them in Pastoral roles, and having a fatherly voice in their lives. Yet now that it's the 21st century does 'sonship' as it is mentioned Biblically still apply?

This book is written to advocate for the application of what I will call the Art of Sonship. As of 2016 (the year of this writing), the generation on the minds, mouths, and studies of most people is that of the Millennial Generation and their effects on the lifestyles and thought-patterns of the generations to come. With them comes words and actions that challenge the traditional structures of church and religion, rejection of the status quo, and the influx of new and radical cultural ideals that seem to cause most to exit the church setting. With a rejection of traditional authority that may come from issues relating to a growing breakdown of the family structure including the father-son relationship along with the advent of technological speed in nearly every aspect of life, we may find foundations as to why this "microwave generation" as some call them is not interested in adopting the Art of Sonship. Why would there be a rejection of sonship in today's modern ministry? The simple answer: sonship takes time.

As one with over 12 years of a ministerial background in a number of leadership roles, I will say that if there is one thing that I have noticed that will not change or be rushed no matter how fast technology advances, that is the Anointing of God. Even as the Bible tells us to lay hands on no man suddenly and to watch those who are prospects for Bishops and Deacons, people, in general, seem to think that ministerial elevation should somehow come quickly. I do have my impatient days as a 34-year-old Millennial myself

"Why would there be a rejection of sonship in today's modern ministry? The simple answer: sonship takes time."

but if I've learned nothing else over my short life, a rush job in ministry is essentially a guarantee that the minister in question will fail in some way.

What is 21st Century Sonship about? It is a cry to Believers, Leaders, Ministerial Fathers and Sons, and Prophetic Voices to get back to mastering the Art of Sonship. What the future holds for us all no one can tell other than the Father who holds time in His hands. But, with so many seeming to be ready to go out and start a ministry, run a business, or jump into marriage all without proper preparation and wise council, the next generation will find themselves looking for Fathers who are not in place because they were never properly raised as sons. So, my friends, as you enjoy this book I will begin it here in the Introduction with the revelation upon which I will end it, Good Sons become Great Fathers. Join me on this journey through sonship, apply the points and revelations to your life, ministry, business, or endeavors and I pray that you will be one who will rise up to see the Sons become the Fathers who will take the Art of Sonship further for the Glory of God.

For [even the whole] creation (all nature) waits expectantly and longs earnestly for God's sons to be made known [waits for the revealing, the disclosing of their sonship].
Romans 8:19 (AMP)

CHAPTER 1 – WHAT IS SONSHIP?

Why do we needs sons? Let's start from a basic and natural perspective. Mankind was created by God with reproductive organs that produce children when a man and woman come together. Humans are set up to be self-replicating when the proper connections are made in that the reproductive process reproduces humans from the foundational DNA of the parental subjects. Without a reproductive process, mankind would cease to exist without getting to another generation. So, simply put, we need sons (children) so that we, as humans, can continue to exist. The same applies to ministries, businesses, royal bloodlines, and more. There needs to be someone to raise and train to take over when the predecessors either depart, retire, or pass away. Without children in place to receive training and guidance then everything that one generation built will die with that generation. Even with someone's family name – traditionally the surname of a family travels with the son and continues on to new generations when the son gets married and has children. However, with a daughter, the surname changes to that of the name of the man she marries and she becomes engrafted into the family line of the husband. Yet in both cases, the bloodline continues and, depending on the family, inheritances can be given to the generations that come as a result of the covenants. The names, bloodlines, traditions, and ancestral inheritances remain because there are children there to receive it and pass it on to their children. From a natural perspective, sons (children) are needed to keep mankind from going extinct and they live out and carry the value systems of their predecessors so that inheritances do not leave the family line.

That said – Why are sons needed in other areas of life such as ministry or business? Without sons (apprentices who can learn the trade of the owner), the entity and practices die with the owner. Pastorally, a ministry will die without sons. In business, the art and practices will die without successors. In royal reigns, the bloodline stops and the throne has to go to someone outside of the intended natural progression. Sons are critical to the life of any endeavor. Part of any good business plan is that of succession planning or exit strategies. They pose the question – who is next to take over? It also shows the training process involved with preparing those who will run the business beyond the current administration. No one else understood this better than Jesus Christ himself. He took 12 disciples and had them walk with him for 3 ½ years to learn, practice, and master his ways. After his resurrection, he took 40 days to show himself as alive and to interact with those who believed. According to Acts 1, he ascended to Heaven but not before giving a final set of instructions that included preaching in Judea, Samaria, and the uttermost parts of the world. He essentially raised and trained spiritual sons, gave them instructions to follow upon his departure, and empowered them with all the tools they would need to succeed while he was gone. If Jesus didn't raise up Apostles and disciples and didn't take the time to train them to continue on when he was gone, we wouldn't know of the Gospel today. Sonship is critical to the continued life of any endeavor.

What is Sonship? Sonship can range in its definitions depending on the situation and the endeavor being approached. For the purpose of this book, sonship will focus on ministry and ministry-related assignments.

Definition of Sonship: *The revelation and understanding of one's assigned purpose to serve a man or woman of God (spiritual father or mother) and the consistent response to assist with building that man or woman's vision that has been given by God.*

Breaking down this ministry-based definition of sonship; it begins as a revelation. A revelation starts as communication with God. Revelations are insights and understandings about God's Word, His being, your purpose, or any wisdom that is attained through a spiritual connection with Him. It comes through times of prayer, reading and studying the Bible, and spending time in the presence of the Almighty God. The word Revelation in Greek verb form is *Apokalupto* and means "to uncover, lay open what has been veiled or covered up; disclose, make bare; to make known, make manifest, disclose what before was unknown [1]." In time spent with the Lord, He will reveal and uncover what was once hidden to you and make known what was once unknown. Before sonship can be claimed or declared, revelation needs to be received.

Sonship is a revelation of one's assigned purpose to serve . . . the key words in the next part of the definition are "purpose" and "serve." Your assignment ultimately comes from the Father but an assignment is going to come out of your purpose. Before declaring yourself to be a son a question needs to be posed of yourself before the Lord: What is your purpose? As prayer goes forth, some serious questions need to be answered relating to why you are where you are and what God's mission is for you to achieve. How many people have signed up for ministry, jobs, marriages, and other major commitments without knowing who they are and what they are doing? When you don't know who you are in Christ and there is a lack of understanding of the true purpose for an endeavor; frustration will manifest. Sonship and ministry commitments should be seen as seriously as marriage. Ideally, before marrying someone, time is taken for the individuals to prepare by getting to know one another; details of expectations are discussed; and overall outcomes are as clear as possible before a lifelong commitment is made. The same applies for sonship. Why should you submit to this man or woman of God? What is the ultimate purpose for committing to this relationship? What are the expected outcomes? Those who miss the purpose of their sonship to someone may get offended with certain requests or with the length of time in service to their leader; especially if the father and son have differing expectations. Take note that the definition continues by saying that there is an assigned purpose to serve. The commitment being made in sonship is a selfless one. Though many lessons will be taught and opportunities given, sonship is about serving the leader for the purpose of glorifying God.

The service of sonship goes to a leader for the purpose of building a vision given to him or her by God. The leader should have the ability to both trust and depend on sons to assist with manifesting what the Lord has given him by way of visions. The definition of sonship is based on Holy Spirit-led selflessness. Sons give up their personal goals for a set of seasons to endeavor to lift up another person's visions. They are assigned to fathers by the Lord to fulfill the Creator's purposes.

While defining what sonship is, there is a need to define what sonship is not. It must be made clear that sonship is not a title, position, or personal pursuit. Some people value titles but a person can have the title of Deacon, Elder, Intercessor, Pastor, or Prophet and still not house the spirit of a son. Neither is sonship a position. It cannot be relegated to a rank among congregations or staff members. Nor is sonship a personal pursuit that is made for selfish gain or notoriety. There are saints out there who find it a source of personal pride to be associated with a well-known leader (not to be confused with being proud of your leader). An arrogant

"Sonship is a matter of the heart. A heart that is submitted to Christ can submit to a leader."

air comes about those that say to themselves that they are sons of this Apostle or that Pastor for the sake of getting people to notice their status and closeness with the leader. Seeking perhaps to one day fill the leader's shoes or branch off into their own endeavor, people with this mindset have lost the true purpose and essence of what it means to be a son as they are blinded by their own personal agendas.

Sonship is a matter of the heart. A heart that is submitted to Christ can submit to a leader. A soul that is saturated by the grace and blood of Jesus Christ can lift up another man's vision over his own. As a son, you love and serve your father through the blood of Jesus. With sonship being such a trusted responsibility, there may be times that sons see weak moments and struggles that the father faces. But it is not a son's job to learn a father's faults but to pray specific prayers of covering and grace that those who are not privy to such details may not be able to do. Sons do not know their fathers by the flesh but by the Spirit. It is the Holy Spirit who constantly guides you and teaches you about your assignment as a son to a father. A son's duties are not based on status or position but are based on what serves the vision of the father in the best way. From cleaning hallways and bathrooms to preaching and teaching, sons only focus on the desire to fulfill the will of God as manifested in the role of the spiritual father.

Continuing the journey into understanding sonship, we must take the time to delve into historical and biblical sonship. The lessons that are gathered in the studies will help us to formulate the view of what 21st Century Sonship should look like and how it should be applied in the ministries of today.

P erhaps the best historical (and somewhat current) example that would emphasize how to see sonship is in the role of the apprentice. Over the generations, many disciplines from shoe making to animal breeding would have the apprentice-to-master learning structure. Essentially, an apprentice is an inexperienced (generally young) person who is looking for an opportunity to work in a field of choice. The treasure that the apprentice is looking for is that of the wisdom and experience that comes from someone who has mastered the trade in which they are interested. Mainly attributed to medieval times [2], the apprenticeship model was performed generally by a young person living with a master craftsman. The apprentice would be paid little or no wages financially but was compensated by way of experience and knowledge. The advantage to the master was that of inexpensive or free daily assistance and someone whom he could train to perform menial tasks and possibly run the business needs of the day. In some countries, during the periods between the 1700s and 1900s, there were guilds that managed the overall apprenticeship process. There were 3 levels to determine the experience and readiness of an individual: Apprentice, Journeyman, and Master. The apprentice, of course, is the most inexperienced level and reflects that the individual is new to the trade. The journeyman may have 3-5 years of experience and would either work in a specific location for his trade or travel elsewhere for further education to exceed his current level of work knowledge in the hopes of mastering his skills. The master, depending on the trade, may have 10-15 years of experience and would have provided the guild with a master project or artwork that proved his mastery of the skill in question. The guild (a group of masters and possibly journeymen) would review the work and determine whether the individual was ready to be called a master and receive acceptance as a part of the guild.

In today's world, although there are some professions that may still follow the apprenticeship model (e.g. plumbers and electricians), we are more likely to identify with the term internship. Internships today allow inexperienced individuals to gain valuable experience by providing time and assistance to a business for little investment on the business' part. One of the major differences in historical apprenticeship and modern-day internship is that of compensation. Many internships of today must be a paid internship to attract quality talent as many people cannot see themselves working somewhere full-time for free. Also, we can see apprenticeship in our society in our educational facilities. Collegiate degrees from Bachelors, to Masters, and on to Ph.D. all show the same initial structure of inexperience up to mastery of a subject.

Biblical Apprenticeship

Biblically, there are some very insightful relationships that can show readers apprenticeship in action. Specifically, using the direct examples of the Moses-to-Joshua and Elijah-to-Elisha relationships we can see not just apprenticeship in operation but the results thereof as the apprentices became masters. In addition, these examples will also reveal more that can be applied to the Art of Sonship.

*"And Moses rose up, **and his minister Joshua**: and Moses went up into*

the mount of God."

Exodus 24:13 (Emphasis added)

The accounts of Moses and Joshua are elaborately detailed in the Pentateuch (the first 5 books of the Bible) and the historical book of Joshua. Moses being the celebrated deliverer of the Israelites from Egyptian captivity and Joshua the militaristic successor who led the nation to the Promised Land and through the many battles required to settle in the territory. How did Joshua get to be the great leader he was destined to be? Other than being God's choice (Deuteronomy 31:7, 17), he was Moses' minister. The word minister in this sense means "servant," in other words he was what we would know today in some church settings as an Armor Bearer. Imagine being that close to Moses during his journey of leading the Children of Israel out of Egypt. Joshua didn't have to wonder about the power of God operating though a man who has faith; he got to see it firsthand. From the declarations of the Lord to Pharoah to let His people go and the parting of the Red Sea to the clouds, thunder, lightning, and flames that would manifest from the presence of God during Moses' discussions with the Creator; Joshua had a front-row seat to all that made up the role of being Israel's leader. But not only did he get to see the glorious days, he was by his side during the frustration that came from the disobedience of the people. Joshua was able to see Moses angry, frustrated, sad, and distraught. He saw him stand before the people judging and hearing every situation one-by-one to be informed of how inefficient his choice was by his father-in-law Jethro. So he saw him make mistakes and learn from those mistakes. He even saw his leader lose out on his visit to the Promised Land due to his uncontrolled anger from striking a rock for water when he was told by the Lord to speak to it. It was Joshua who was on the Mount near Moses when he heard the cries of the people as they were worshipping a golden calf because they thought their leader was taking too long to show back up. Joshua's intimate experience with Moses' accomplishments and failures prepared him for his own leadership role. Ultimately, Joshua is a great example of biblical apprenticeship in that he learned directly from his leader.

"Joshua's intimate experience with Moses' accomplishments and failures prepared him for his own leadership role."

"So he departed thence, and ***found Elisha the son of Shaphat****, who was plowing with twelve yoke of oxen before him, and he with the twelfth:* ***and Elijah passed by him, and cast his mantle upon him.****"*

1 Kings 19:19 (Emphasis added)

As another example of apprenticeship in the Bible, Elisha as an apprentice to Elijah provides excellent detail. Elijah, one of the greatest historical Prophets, is famously known for the miracles he performed and his battle with the evil manifested in the form of Israel's King and Queen, Ahab and Jezebel. He was truly a master of prophetics and the miracle-working power behind the Lord's mantle that is given to the Office of the Prophet. In continuing this discussion of apprenticeship, Elijah's protégé Elisha had some of the same points as Joshua with Moses. Elisha was chosen by God to be Elijah's successor and he walked with the Prophet closely to see the Lord work directly through the man of God. Perhaps the most powerful point of Elisha's apprenticeship is found in 2 Kings 2. After his time of training (some theologians believe he spent about 10 years serving Elijah) Elisha was presented with an opportunity. Elijah asked him what he wanted to have him do before he was taken away by the Lord. Elisha asks for a double-portion of Elijah's spirit; Elijah then says that although it's a hard thing that was asked, if he sees him go up then it shall be given. How many apprentices get such an opportunity? Most apprenticeships end with a head full of knowledge and experience and a handshake out of the door. But this one ended with a spiritual impartation of great magnitude. Not only did Elisha get to see his master taken up but his request was fully granted. If one would take a moment to count the amount of miracles that the Prophets performed during their ministries, it would be found that Elisha did exactly twice as many miracles as Elijah. That is truly effective apprenticeship. If a master would raise a trainee to be able to do double of what he was able to perform then the time spent mentoring was definitely effective. More will be shared in later chapters regarding the Moses-Joshua and Elijah-Elisha relationships but the initial view of apprenticeship and the results of their time of training show just how important times of learning are for successful sonship and leadership.

To this point, majority of the discussion on sonship and apprenticeship has been historical. So what do we face in the 21st century regarding the Art of Sonship? In a previous book, Ministering to Millennials: The Challenges of Reaching Generation "Why [3]," issues that the Millennial Generation currently face are discussed such as how their relationship with the church seems to be waning. Easily, the factor that sets this generation and the ones to come apart from previous generations is the advent of technology. 81% of the Millennial Generation is on Facebook with an average of 250 friends which is much higher than their counterparts in previous generations. Beyond social media, technological advances in communication, travel, cooking, business, and nearly every avenue of life has caused a general expectation of immediate gratification among those living in modern countries. Take a moment to imagine the child back in the 1700s with a 60-year-old master who now has access to all the information he could need to not only make the old man's wisdom obsolete but can cut the child's learning time by at least 75% with a few good YouTube videos. He will grow immediately disinterested and disengaged because the grown man is not saying anything the child can't just look up in less than 3 seconds. The discussions that start with "Back in my day when I was growing up" result in a teenage eye-roll as the protégé stares out of the window waiting on a response to his text. This thought pattern and mindset is what the modern-day church is up against. It's not that the younger generation age 35 and below isn't willing to work hard or devote some time to a task, they just want to be able to understand why.

For instance, why should a young man choose the path toward a career as a steel worker in a factory that may max out at a $40,000 salary after 25-30 years of hard work when he can go online, spend a year learning how to program, make an addictive app for Android and iPhone, and make that same $40,000 in 2 months after his app posts to Google Play through advertiser endorsements? Or why would a young lady marry at 20 to the first guy she meets that has a decent job when she can go to eHarmony and sift through a few million profiles of eligible bachelors who may (or may not) be the better catch? Why should a high school graduate go to a 4-year college, and rack up a mountain of student loan debt, just to get a degree that not only may be obsolete by graduation but doesn't guarantee a job when he could just go learn a trade directly from a 2-year college and start his own business with minimal debt? The 21st century young person has more options and pathways than any other comparable person in the previous generations. Along with these options, they are at a point where credentials, jobs, food, information, and almost anything they can think of comes quickly and without much work.

With that said, in relation to apprenticeship and sonship – Why would the modern-day young person be interested in such an antiquated model? When you tell someone in the 21st century that they have to invest time and show themselves faithful over the course of 5 to 10 years you may hear an indignant gasp and a look of horror coming your way. Why? Because in the 21st century time is a commodity that people realize just cannot be wasted. Investing time is risky business. Back in the 1800s a person could invest time just sitting at home reading novels or working with a mentor to gain his thought pattern on how to bake some bread in just the right way. Today, because there are so many options, we need to know up front how much time something will take and what is expected of us during the timeframe. In Corporate America, there is a great difference between the Baby Boomer and the Millennial when it comes to work. The Baby Boomer is fine with coming to work, doing an excellent job, and going home with the satisfaction of a job well done. The Millennial, typically after a year or two in the same role, will start getting bored and asking "What's next?" Or if they are expected to continue in the same area, they need to see some financial increase and some serious promotion potential. Wasting time is not an option for newer generations. Endeavors need to seem meaningful, purposeful, and, most of all, profitable for self-reward and self-recognition.

"To truly understand how the Art of Sonship must be applied to the newer generations we must know that there has to be a level of engagement that has not been seen prior to their arrival."

All of this said, the constant question in the mind of a 21st century apprentice, whether vocalized or not, is going to be "Why?" To truly understand how the Art of Sonship must be applied to the newer

generations we must know that there has to be a level of engagement that has not been seen prior to their arrival. Time cannot be wasted nor can there be much by way of inaccuracy in the trade in question. However, how do you also instill the power of patience into a young person? Or the responsibility of delayed gratification to those who have instant access to so much else? In the arena of ministry, not only does this take prayer but sound teaching on the strategic art of waiting on the Lord for manifestations and for the quiet voice of the Holy Spirit needs to be engrained in the minds and hearts of a generation so eager to jump out and make a name for themselves.

For [even the whole] creation (all nature) waits expectantly and longs earnestly
for God's sons to be made known [waits for the revealing, the disclosing of their
sonship].
Romans 8:19 (AMP)

Is the newest generation interested in "mastering" a trade or serving under a master for a long period of time to ensure success in a given area of discipline? Despite what may be popular opinion, there may be more support to believe that this generation desires to be excellent and well known for something; they may just see the ways of the previous generations as antiquated and they await more efficient and effective ways of achieving mastery. The question of the hour would then be:

Does the newest generation have any interest in true Sonship?

As mentioned in the introduction, real sonship takes time. The irony being that the time sonship takes to fully run its course takes time that the newest generations would argue that they don't have. As they balance careers, colleges, families, and other endeavors, the disposable time of a busy young person is low to non-existent. When does a family of 5 with both parents working, getting children to soccer practice and cheerleading camp, and attempting to finish doctorates through their online colleges so they can get promoted have time to sit quietly and pray to hear God? What about the college student taking 7 classes this semester who is the

President of his fraternity and does community service each week; when does he have time to follow his Pastor around to learn more about ministry? The truth is that the many activities that take up our time can be distractions from taking the time out to do as Jesus did and pray to the Father for direction and guidance. If we don't have time (or think we don't have time) to pray even just to ask God for His direction and protection, our priorities are misdirected. This is not to say that we won't be busy even when we're in the vein of exactly what the Lord has for us but we will know beyond any doubt that we are doing everything that He has ordained for our lives and nothing more.

In the arena of ministry, sonship takes time and a great deal of it. To learn the intricacies of how to hear the Lord and enact what He desires while also working with people who may or may not be operating in the Spirit of the Lord takes much wisdom that only comes with time at the feet of someone who has been there. A term that is tossed around about the newer generations is "Microwave Generation." The microwave has been a time-saving invention that is now a household item that most people couldn't imagine living without. Zapping a pre-made meal and having it ready in 3-minutes versus cooking from scratch and taking 2 hours to prepare one meal for a family seems to win the battle every time among busy people. Yet the mindset that seems to be transferring is that the microwave technology should apply to every other area of life. Could you imagine a microwave marriage? A man and woman coming together in marriage after just a month of courtship could be a disaster (not that it hasn't worked before). There are so many things, big and small, to know about a person before committing your life and saying all that you are is going to that person. From belief systems to the way they pop gum as they chew; no one can fully know a person in a microwave time setting to the point of truly knowing what you're getting into. In that same case, preparing oneself in ministry and to minister before the Lord takes time that just cannot be negated.

"Faithfulness to the Lord and commitment to an endeavor is not shown in a moment of talent but over a long period of consistency through a number of seasons."

1 Timothy 5:22 says "Lay hands suddenly on no man, neither be partaker of other men's sins: keep thyself pure." And 1 Timothy 3:6, speaking of those interested in becoming Pastors or Bishops, gives as one of the requirements "Not a novice, lest being lifted up with pride he fall into the condemnation of the devil." In other words, to grow in ministry, time (and plenty of it) is one of the deciding factors as to whether a person is truly ready to move forward. Why is time such an important factor in sonship? The answer is relatively simple: Faithfulness to the Lord and commitment to an endeavor is not shown in a moment of talent but over a long period of consistency through a number of seasons. That's exactly why most corporations have a probationary period of 90-days before a new

employee is allowed to access valuable benefits. 3 months, from a working perspective, is a good amount of time for an employer to get an initial gauge as to what kind of worker has joined their ranks. They can see if the person shows up on-time consistently, has a good attitude, and whether they are a good fit for the corporation. After 90-days the employees can access benefits and perhaps they have completed some type of training that makes them a full-fledged associate of the corporation. Now, here's where things get interesting. How much time should pass before a person should be considered for a promotion? In corporate environments, most may say that you need to have worked in your current position for 1-2 years before you can even apply. There are also behavioral stipulations that may say that the person applying cannot have had any negative reports relating to performance or interaction over the previous year. In addition to those requirements, there may be further stipulations depending on the level of responsibility for the position. There are security clearances for those dealing with sensitive information. There are credit checks for those in management and finance. And there are stockholder and Board of Director reviews, audits, and interviews for those asking for executive-level positions. These positions do not come easily either; the employer reviews and verifies educational information, criminal histories, employment tenures, and more. The positions that pay the most will require of the applicant years, if not at least a decade, of experience in a certain area. The overall point being, if we see that secular employers take the time to perform due diligence on potential candidates expecting from them years of consistency and high-level performance, why should the Body of Christ expect anything less of those desiring to lead and represent the Lord? Sonship, like corporate expectations, needs to come with the mindset of time along with consistent positive performance will lead to ministerial opportunity (as declared by the Spirit of the Lord).

Attaining the Anointing of the Lord

Now, up to this point, this chapter has spoken of 21st Century Sonship in terms of a natural comparison to what we see and may relate to on a day-to-day basis. The major point of time and the specialized art of waiting patiently on one's turn and time is an underlying message that all generations can receive. Yet, this discussion would be remiss if there wasn't some emphasis placed on the spiritual points of sonship and just how important they are in the walk of the son to a father. Specifically, in the midst of all of the natural things a person can do while training for his next place in the Lord; one thing that any saint cannot afford to go forth without is the Anointing of the Lord. The Hebrew word for Anoint is "Mashach" and means "To smear, to anoint (as in consecration), to spread a liquid [4]." The entry for "Anointing" in Smith's Bible Dictionary [5] says the following:

Anointing, in Holy Scripture, is either, I. Material--with oil--or II. Spiritual--with the Holy Ghost.

I. MATERIAL:

1) Ordinary: Anointing the body or head with oil was a common practice with the Jews, as with other Oriental nations. (Ruth 3:3 ; Micah 6:15) Anointing the head with oil or ointment seems also to have been a mark of respect sometimes paid by a host to his guests. (Luke 7:46 and Psalm 23:5)

2) Official: It was a rite of inauguration into each of the three typical offices of the Jewish commonwealth.

   a. Prophets were occasionally anointed to their office, (1 Kings 19:16) and were called messiahs, or anointed. (1 Chronicles 16:22 ; Psalms 105:15)

   b. Priests, at the first institution of the Levitical priesthood, were all anointed to their offices, (Exodus 40:15; Numbers 3:3) but afterwards anointing seems to have been specially reserved for the high priest, (Exodus 29:29; Leviticus 16:32) so that "the priest that is anointed," (Leviticus 4:3) is generally thought to mean the high priest.

   c. Kings. Anointing was the principal and divinely-appointed ceremony in the inauguration of the Jewish Kings. (1 Samuel 9:16, 10:1; 1 Kings 1:34, 39) The rite was sometimes performed more than once. David was thrice anointed.

    d. Inanimate objects also were anointed with oil, in token of their being set apart for religious service. Thus Jacob anointed a pillar at Bethel. (Genesis 31:13; Exodus 30:26-28)

3) Ecclesiastical: Anointing with oil is prescribed by St. James to be used for the recovery of the sick. (James 5:14) Analogous to this is the anointing with oil practiced by the twelve. (Mark 6:13)

II. SPIRITUAL:

4) In the Old Testament a Deliverer is promised under the title of Messiah, or Anointed, (Psalms 2:2; Daniel 9:25-26) and the nature of his anointing is described to be spiritual, with the Holy Ghost. (Isaiah 61:1) see Luke 4:18. In the New Testament Jesus of Nazareth is shown to be the Messiah, or Christ or Anointed, of the Old Testament, (John 1:41; Acts 9:22; Acts 17:2-3; Acts 18:4, 28) and the historical fact of his being anointed with the Holy Ghost is asserted and recorded. (John 1:32-33; Acts 4:27; 10:38) Christ was anointed as prophet, priest, and king.

5) Spiritual anointing with the Holy Ghost is conferred also upon Christians by God. (2 Corinthians 1:21) "Anointing" expresses the sanctifying influences of the Holy Spirit upon Christians who are priests and kings unto God.

Ultimately, the anointing is a process in which the vessel is set apart for service to the Lord. You may recall the initial anointing of David by the Prophet Samuel as explained in 1 Samuel chapter 16. All of Jesse's sons were called forth to stand before the Prophet but the Lord said No to each one until David was brought before him. Take note of what verses 11-13 say:

And Samuel said unto Jesse, Are here all thy children? And he said, There remaineth yet the youngest, and, behold, he keepeth the sheep. And Samuel said unto Jesse, Send and fetch him: for we will not sit down till he come hither. And he sent, and brought him in. Now he was ruddy, and withal of a beautiful countenance, and goodly to look to. **And the LORD said, Arise, anoint him: for this is he. Then Samuel took the horn of oil, and anointed him in the midst of his brethren: and the Spirit of the LORD came upon David from that day forward.** *So Samuel rose up, and went to Ramah.*
1 Samuel 16:11-13 (Emphasis added)

There is much that can be discussed in this chapter regarding David but there is a need to focus in on the fact that not only was he chosen of the Lord to be the next King of Israel but he was *anointed* in the midst of witnesses for his next assignment. Why is this so important? 1 Timothy 4:14 says "Neglect not the gift that is in thee, which was given thee by prophecy, with **the laying on of the hands of the presbytery."** The process of the anointing and the laying on of hands as mentioned by Paul to Timothy stirs up and activates the spiritual gifts that are within you. The scripture shown in 1 Samuel 16 says that the Spirit of the Lord came upon David from that day forward. Imagine if David attempted to become King without the Spirit of the Lord, without someone recognizing his gifts, or without being anointed to fulfill his assignment; not only would failure have been the most likely result but there isn't a guarantee that the Lord would have empowered him to finish any endeavor he faced.

That, arguably, is the biggest challenge facing the generation that is raised on technology and quick results – The challenge of waiting to be anointed, confirmed, and activated by the laying on of hands by a true ministerial master. Each son (Joshua, Elisha, David, Timothy, and others) was proven over time before they were activated. Joshua served as Moses' minister (more than likely for the entire 40-years that Israel was in the wilderness); Elisha served Elijah for at least 10 years based on what most theologians believe (there are differing answers); David faced his own battles and raised sheep before receiving the anointing and killing Goliath; and Timothy walked with Paul for years before being sent off to Pastor in Ephesus. Each son in the 21st century should learn from these examples before launching into an endeavor. Going without the anointing of a father means that the son is trusting in his own strength to accomplish a mission that only God can complete.

Appointment vs. Self-Promotion

If you look across the Internet and search for churches, Pastors, or ministries you will find a countless number of websites, blogs, and words posted inviting one and all to join in building a vision sent by God. Have you ever seen all of these ministries and wondered where they came from or how they were started? Some have some stories of honorable yet humble beginnings of trusting the Lord, standing on His Word, and 30 years later, here they are as one of the most well-known ministries. Some are just starting out, seeking funding and support, and preaching excellent words as fresh voices on the scene. Yet there are also some that may not be as well put together or as forth coming. They may boast a name without history or exalt a doctrine that doesn't line up with scripture. Just as with the real estate market, ministry seeking is definitely a "buyer beware" situation.

Perhaps one of the most interesting things out there on the Internet is Online Ordination and Instant Online Ministry Credentials. For a fee, you can get some random company out there to print off an official-looking document with glimmering seals and wonderful fonts saying that you, are officially ordained to "Preach the Gospel," perform weddings, officiate communion, and facilitate funerals. Can't you imagine an infomercial on TV saying: "Yes YOU – For the low, low price of {insert price here} you can be ordained! No lines, no waiting, and none of the patience required to let a spiritual father sign-off on your ministry! But wait, there's more! For just $20 more you can get your Ph.D. in Hermeneutical Studies. Yes, YOU can be Dr. {Insert Your Name} instantly!!! No student loans, no 4 to 8 years of study and sacrifice. Just sign up, send your money, and you'll be credentialed and ready to do ministry TOMORROW!" While we can be facetious in our presentation of the concept, this is a truly serious matter that must be addressed and covered in prayer.

Imagine that my friends, a bunch of 'ministers' out there with 21st century technology falsifying their credentials and, even worse, FALSFYING THE ANOINTING! The Bible warns us in various passages about false Apostles and false Prophets (2 Cor. 11, Rev. 2:1-3, 2 Peter 2). The falseness doesn't just apply to those who are completely opposite of the Gospel such as witches, psychics, atheists, and sorcerers; but they apply to those who claim to be preachers, ministers, and sons but in reality they have not been vetted by reputable sources in the Body of Christ to prove that they are who they say they are (Ref. Jude). The 21st century has brought with it not just the technology to do great things more efficiently for the Lord but also has made it much easier for those who are not willing to do the work to falsify credentials and attempt to move forth without the anointing.

With that said, it is necessary that we are all appointed by the Lord and confirmed by the people that He has set in place to accurately judge our readiness and not self-promoted because we are too impatient to allow God to complete the work He is doing in us. When you are appointed like David, the Lord is honor-bound to keep you and protect you if you will obey Him. However, if you promote yourself, the Lord is not with you and whatever attacks that ensue from satanic opposition are not His responsibility to wave off because you moved without His blessing (Ref. Numbers 14:39-45).

T he Bible itself is our foundation for everything that the Lord would have us to learn regarding His will and His ways. The topic of sonship is no different. The following examples of sonship come from the Bible and will highlight both positive and negative instances for reference.

Positive Sonship

Paul and Sons (Timothy and Titus) – The Books of 1 and 2 Timothy and Titus

Paul's overall story is a familiar one. Known as an Apostle to the Gentiles, Paul spent time on missionary journeys establishing churches as outlined in the books of Acts and the Pauline Epistles. Regarding sonship, however, Paul specifically calls out 2 men whom he gives the title "Son" – Timothy and Titus. In the letters written directly to them he called Timothy his "True Son in the Faith" and his "Dear Son" and called Titus his "True Son in our common faith." Both men were trained by Paul and were directly involved in his ministry. Neither of them stayed in general service to the Apostle, they both were consecrated as Bishops over specific areas – Titus over Crete and Timothy over Ephesus.

Sonship Points to Note:

- Paul spiritually raised Timothy and Titus
- They both served in roles that were a direct benefit to Paul's ministry
- Paul saw potential in them and, when the time came, set them in place as Bishops

- Timothy and Titus followed Paul as sons until their father said it was time for them to lead

Noah and Sons (Shem and Japheth) – Genesis 9:18-29

After the receding of the worldwide flood and the establishment of the Noahic Covenant, Noah had a moment when he got drunk and feel asleep naked. When Shem and Japheth found out from Ham what happened they took a garment and methodically walked backwards so that they would not see his nakedness while they got him covered up.

Sonship Points to Note:

- Noah, like any human being, had a moment of weakness and exposure
- Shem and Japheth did not even allow themselves to look at their father in a weakened and exposed state
- They did not go and tell anyone else about his weakness or nakedness
- They could be trusted with the sensitive and personal information
- In Noah's exposed state, Shem and Japheth immediately covered their father without so much as acknowledging his nakedness until he was composed enough to hear their account of the event
- True sons cover their fathers if they are privy to moments of weakness and keep sensitive information to themselves

Elijah and Elisha – 1 Kings 19, 2 Kings 2

Elijah is famously known as the great Prophet who faced off with Jezebel and led the fire-filled standoff against false prophets at Mount Carmel. Told by the Lord that Elisha would take his place in 1 Kings 19, he found him, placed his mantle upon him, and the protégé followed him until the day Elijah was taken up. It is believed by some theologians that Elisha followed Elijah for 10 years prior to taking his place. Elijah performed 16 miracles during his prophetic tenure. Elisha asked for a double portion and, as a result, performed 32 miracles during his lifetime; exactly double that of his spiritual father.

Sonship Points to Note:

- Elisha's service to Elijah was not a short period of time
- Elisha's faithfulness as a son blessed him to be able to do double the miracles of his father

Jesus and John – Luke 3

Jesus and John, in the natural, were cousins but spiritually, John submitted to Jesus and gave full recognition to who he is as the Lamb of God and the Savior of mankind. As powerful as John was as a Prophet he declared that he wasn't even worthy to unlatch Jesus' shoes and that he must decrease so that Christ can increase. John spiritually paved the way for Jesus by preaching the will of God.

Sonship Points to Note:

- John submitted to Jesus as the greater between the two of them

- John recognized who Jesus was, not just to the world, but specifically to him

- John did not try to overstep Jesus or take any glory for himself

- John knew who he was and was comfortable in submitting to the will of Jesus

- John's work was for the purpose of building another man's kingdom and reputation, not his own

Eli and Samuel: 1 Samuel 3

Samuel was given back to the Lord by his parents and served in the temple with Eli as his tutor and Priest. He learned from Eli how to run and maintain the temple while also gaining understanding of the voice and ways of God. As a boy, he heard directly from the Lord who told him of things to come. Samuel grew to become a great Prophet who installed Kings and judged the people of God.

Sonship Points to Note:

- Samuel grew under the tutelage of a Priest of God

- When he heard the voice of God, he first ran to his spiritual father for confirmation and verification

- His spiritual father told him that he was hearing from God

- His spiritual father gave him directions on how to interact with God and what to say the next time he heard the Lord's voice

- Even though Samuel heard from God for himself, he interacted with his spiritual father to get wisdom and direction

- Before prophesying to Eli (his covering and the man who is his spiritual father), he was given permission to release what he heard; he did not prophesy to someone of higher authority without permission

Moses and Joshua – The Books of Exodus, Numbers, and Deuteronomy

Joshua was Moses' minister, which means he was his direct servant – What we would know today as an Armor Bearer. Joshua was nearby during major and minor events watching Moses lead the Children of Israel out of Egypt to his dying day. He also fought wars in support of Israel and in belief of Moses as a man who heard from God. Joshua grew to replace Moses as Israel's leader and led them in to the Promised Land.

Sonship Points to Note:

- Joshua was a military leader who submitted to Moses as a spiritual father and learned more about God by watching his leader's interaction with both the Lord and the people.

- Joshua had a committed position that directly served the Israelite leader

- Joshua both fought for and led others to fight for Moses and the vision of God to get Israel to the Promised Land

- Joshua believed God so much that he was only 1 of 2 out of his entire generation to agree with Israel's ability to attain the Promise. He and Caleb were the only ones of his age group to make it see the Promised Land.

- Joshua never defied Moses but absorbed many lessons just by watching. When he became the leader he knew God was with him just as He was with Moses yet there were some strategies that he remembered and changed when he took over (e.g. Moses sent out 12 spies only to get 2 who agreed with God; Joshua only sent 2 spies as a strategy difference).

Negative Sonship

Moses and Korah – Numbers 16

Korah, as a son under the overall leadership of Moses, led a revolt against him. Ultimately saying that he and others hear from God, he challenged the Prophet for his seat of power of Israel. Upon standing before the Lord and the Creator confirming Korah's defiance; he and all of his followers were swallowed up by the earth never to be heard from again.

Sonship Points to Note:

- Korah was full of pride and was not humble enough to submit to God's choice in Moses

- Korah's lack of submission to Moses represented a greater lack of submission to God and His will

- Korah wanted power and found like-minded people in the camp to follow his plan
- Korah's death not only showed that he was out of order but that God does not tolerate those who are supposed to be believers rising up against those whom He chose to lead His people.

Samuel and sons (Joel and Abiah) – 1 Samuel 8:1-6

Samuel grew to be one of the greatest Prophets to ever live but his sons somehow grew to only desire financial gain. According to 1 Samuel 8:1-3, they were made judges but became corrupt as they only went after money by taking bribes and perverting judgment through greed. It was so bad to the point that the Elders of Israel pointed it out to Samuel and asked for a King like the other nations.

Sonship Points to Note:

- Even sons who are directly connected with anointed fathers can choose ungodly paths
- Sons have the potential to corrupt God's plans and cause the People of God to take another plan

Eli and sons (Hophni and Phineas) – 1 Samuel 4

Eli may have been a good Priest but his failure in fatherhood allowed his sons to grow in corruption while also causing a curse on his family line. Hophni and Phineas would oppress the people that would come in to sacrifice to the Lord by taking some of the offerings for themselves.

They would violate the women that came to worship through fornication and cause the Israelites to turn away from making sacrifices to the Lord because of their horrific actions. Ultimately, in a war with the Philistines, both sons were killed and the ark of God was taken. When Eli heard the news he fell to his death bringing an end to his bloodline.

Sonship Points to Note:

- Ministerial Sonship requires integrity
- Sonship is an extremely sensitive position that requires the son to be trusted
- Sons who violate trust cause contempt among the people with the Priesthood and with God
- Sons represent God and their fathers
- Sons without Godly integrity can only bring shame to the name of the Lord and the name of the father

Noah and Son (Ham) – Genesis 9:18-29

After the receding of the worldwide flood and the establishment of the Noahic Covenant, Noah had a moment when he got drunk and feel asleep naked. Ham was the first to see Noah as he laid there exposed. Instead of covering him as his brothers did, he ran and told Shem and Japheth what he saw while allowing his exposure to remain.

Sonship Points to Note:

- Sons, while walking with fathers, may see moments of human weakness and frailty
- Sons should be able to be trusted with weak moments

- True sons will always cover their fathers
- Ham ran and told his brothers what happened and looked at Noah's nakedness
- Fathers should not have to be concerned with whether a son will gossip about sensitive moments and information

Paul and Demas – 2 Timothy 4:10

2 Timothy 4:10 speaks of a former disciple named Demas who forsook Paul and left him stranded. The simple reason for doing so was that he loved the present world. As a trusted son, Demas, whom Paul allowed to walk closely with him, left the Apostle at a critical moment during his ministry. The world and its pleasures overtook Demas and required Paul to reach out to Timothy, a son he could trust, to come and assist him further.

Sonship Points to Note:
- Fathers should be able to lean on their sons in times of trouble and need
- Sons must choose, far ahead of critical seasons, what path they will take: Christ or the world
- When sons are out of place, fathers are left to struggle with fulfilling their visions
- A son who walks in the flesh can never truly support a father who walks by the Spirit

Elisha and Gehazi – 2 Kings 4 and 5

Gehazi served as Elisha's assistant and, essentially, a prophetic son. He worked well with the mighty Prophet until the healing of Naaman was completed. When Elisha refused to take payment for the healing of the Lord, Gehazi went behind his back and used his authority and association as a son to get Naaman to give some resources into his hands. Gehazi lied in the name of the Prophet Elisha and completely misrepresented him and the Lord. Having seen everything via the Spirit of the Lord, Elisha confronted Gehazi and he was struck with leprosy for the rest of his life. In addition, the leprosy would not stop with him, according to 2 Kings 5:26 his seed would also be leprous. As a result of his greed, he cursed himself and his bloodline.

Sonship Points to Note:

- Sons are not just trusted with tasks and activities, they are trusted with their father's name and reputation
- Authority and elevation are given just for being a son to a father who is known and respected
- The character of the son must be impeccable, every action is a reflection on the father
- Misrepresentation of the father and the Lord is one of the highest offences that a son can commit

Birthrights

In addition to the examples presented there is a biblical and historical concept that all sons should understand and apply to their spiritual walk; that of the Birthright.

What is a Birthright? According to Easton's Bible Dictionary [6]:

> This word denotes the special privileges and advantages belonging to the first-born son among the Jews. He became the priest of the family. The first-born son had allotted to him also a double portion of the paternal inheritance. The first-born inherited the judicial authority of his father, whatever it might be.

Smith's Bible Dictionary [7] explains that the rights of those with the birthright are:

(1) The functions of the priesthood in the family with the paternal blessing.

(2) A "double portion" of the paternal property was allotted by the Mosaic law.

(3) The eldest son succeeded to the official authority of the father. The first-born of the king was his successor by law.

And the International Standard Bible Encyclopedia [8] says:

> Birthright is the right which naturally belonged to the firstborn son. Where there were more wives than one, the firstborn was the son who in point of time was born before the others, apparently whether his mother was a wife or a concubine.

The birthright of the firstborn consisted in the first place of a double portion of what his father had to leave. This probably means that he had a double share of such property as could be divided. We have no certain knowledge of the manner in which property was inherited in the patriarchal age, but it seems probable that the lands and flocks which were the possession of the family as a whole, remained so after the death of the father.

The firstborn became head of the family and thus succeeded to the charge of the family property, becoming responsible for the maintenance of the younger sons, the widow or widows, and the unmarried daughters. He also, as head, succeeded to a considerable amount of authority over the other members. Further, he generally received the blessing, which placed him in close and favored covenant-relationship with Yahweh.

The birthright is an extremely important part of sonship. In the times of the patriarchs, the birthright would guarantee blessings, resources, and authority for the firstborn son. In the case of Reuben, the firstborn of Jacob, he lost his birthright because he defiled his father's bed. The birthright was ultimately transferred to Joseph (1 Chronicles 5:1-2). And, in hunger, Esau sold his birthright to Jacob for food (Genesis 25:29-34). He apparently did not understand what he was giving up. In addition to the birthrights came the blessings of being the firstborn son upon which the fathers would pronounce a blessing that would empower the son for the purpose of being the head of the family and leader of his tribe. In the midst of trickery, Isaac blessed Jacob with the blessing that was originally for Esau. That blessing guaranteed his elevation based on the blessings of Abraham (Genesis 27 and 28).

The purpose in understanding the birthright and the blessings is that they apply in the 21st century relationship of spiritual fathers to spiritual sons. The major difference is that a son does not have to be a father's firstborn to receive the birthright and blessings. Because Christ is the firstborn of the Heavenly Father (John 3:16) and the firstborn of the dead (Colossians 1:15-19) and we are Joint-Heirs with Jesus Christ (Romans 8:16-17) we are also in place to receive the same blessings because of our Lord's blood sacrifice. Thanks to Christ, we can receive from our spiritual fathers the blessings and mantles that come with their Offices like Elisha received from Elijah, we can receive a spiritual impartation that empowers us for our ministries like Paul gave to Timothy and Titus, and we can be anointed by the oil of the Lord for our predestined positions in Christ just like David was anointed by Samuel. We do not have to worry if we are not our spiritual father's firstborn because, just as with Joseph's sons Manasseh and Ephraim, there is not a limit as to who receives the birthright or blessing. You can be the younger of the list of sons and yet still receive a birthright that is all your own without limitations. The key is faithfulness to the call that Christ has given and when the time comes for blessing among the sons, the power of the Lord will individually bless all those who have served with a heart that glorifies Him.

Purity in Sonship

But Jehoshaphat said, Is there not here a prophet of the Lord, that we may enquire of the Lord by him? And one of the king of Israel's servants answered and said, Here is Elisha the son of Shaphat, **which poured water on the hands of Elijah.**

2 Kings 3:11 (emphasis added)

As a final point among the biblical examples and points of sonship, there must be a purity among all sons as they walk before their fathers. Ministerial sons, especially those that walk closely to their fathers in roles like those of the Armor Bearer, must be sure to purify themselves often before the Lord Jesus. This is done by consistently staying away from sin and evil, refusing to entertain demonic spirits, and confessing sins to Jesus Christ and allowing the blood to cover any and all points of life. Why is this important? Because those who walk closely with fathers are called to pour water on the hands of their fathers. The water represents 3 things: 1) The Word of God, 2) Purity that covers and cleanses the father, and 3) A spiritual walk that does not taint the father, his spiritual state, or his reputation.

The Water as the Word of God: Sons must grow to be well versed in the Word of God. The Bible is the foundation for the faith of all believers. Without knowing the Word a son can be tossed by the trials of life and the persecution that can arise by being associated with a ministerial father. No one washes their hands with dirty water but with pure and clean-looking water. It is up to the son to study to show himself approved so that his understanding of the Word is ready like iron to sharpen the iron of others, including the father.

<u>The Water as Purity</u>: Sons must be able, available, and willing to cover and cleanse the atmosphere surrounding the father. Just as Nehemiah did not come before the King with a sad countenance, sons must be peaceable and wise in the presence of their fathers doing their absolute best to be an uplifting part of their lives. Only those who are pure can do this effectively. The key word is pure, not perfect. Biblical perfection is equated to maturity. The perfection of

"All who claim sonship have the responsibility to keep the water they offer to the Lord and the father clean and pure."

being sinless only belongs to Christ. However, we do have a responsibility to keep our hands clean as we touch the holy things that fathers would require from sons. Constantly keeping sins confessed to Christ and pleading the blood of Jesus over our lives will keep us pure before the Lord and thus pure before the fathers.

<u>The Water as a Spiritual Walk</u>: The spiritual walk of a son on a daily basis not only represents the Heavenly Father but also the spiritual father. Sons who are recognized as being those who are close to a father are automatically in a place of needed discipline. Sons of a Man of God

cannot be seen everywhere doing everything that their worldly counterparts are doing. In the same vein, there is a level of trust that comes with sonship. Sons may interact more often than others with their father's family and friends. Being wise and meticulous when socially engaging those who are near and dear to the father is critical to being a trusted son. Recall Gehazi's selfish interaction with Naaman. In that case the son risked Elisha's relationship with Naaman and his prophetic reputation by seeking to gain finances from the man whom God healed. Elisha was not trying to be 'paid' for performing a miracle that came from the Lord Himself and he was not trying to get any glory for Naaman's healing. Gehazi's actions were more than a simple act of selfishness. As a son walking with an Internationally-known Prophet, his actions carried much more weight – Not because of who he was but because of who his father was.

Pouring water on the hands of the father is a key responsibility of sons. Whether the son walks closely or occasionally serves in various capacities, all who claim sonship have the responsibility to keep the water they offer to the Lord and the father clean and pure.

A s important as it is to know how to operate as a son it is just as important (especially for fathers) to know how to recognize whether a son is a true (God-sent) son or a false (self-focused) son.

The Attributes of a True Son

1) True sons have a proper view of their spiritual father

What is meant by a "proper view?" True sons know who their spiritual father is but do not put him on a pedestal on which no human being should be set. No Pastor, Minister, Apostle, Prophet, or any other servant in the Kingdom of God should be held so highly as to negate their humanity. They are not God, Jesus, Holy Spirit, or some supremely special angelic being sent from the heavens. Each father is a human like any other. They need the blood of Jesus to wash away their sins just like any other person and it is unfair to them (and Christ) to place them on a heavenly stage as if they can't do wrong. True sons recognize this. They respect and honor the office and anointing that the vessel walks in but do not worship him or her. They serve with excellence as if they are serving the Lord Jesus Himself but understand that the father, who hears from the Lord, is a servant of the Lord as well.

Sons are assigned by the Lord to serve a spiritual father. If the father ever deviates from the course of Christ or departs from Kingdom purposes, the son's assignment to the father is no longer valid although the love of Christ should always remain. Sonship is based on Kingdom purpose and principles. If Christ is not the center and purpose of the father/son relationship then, from a ministerial perspective, the relationship is merely a working partnership or friendship on the human level. However, when Christ is the center, the son is connected to the father for a season of purpose (the time limit is set by the Heavenly Father) in which the son is there to assist with building the father's vision while also gleaning knowledge, wisdom, and key lessons that can be applied for further purposes.

2) True sons pray specifically for the father, the father's family, and the father's Kingdom purpose

Sons, as part of their basic role and assignment, are intercessors. True sons will take the time to pray and fast both for and with the father for the sake of covering and defending all that God plans to manifest in the

True sons are intercessors

father's life and ministry. True sons hear the voice of God and respond through prayer and obedient faithfulness to the Spirit of the Lord. In addition, in the natural realm, sons grow to learn to anticipate the needs of the father they serve while also staying in order and wisely not overstepping proper boundaries.

3) True sons respond to the father's voice

In John 10, Jesus speaks about the sheep that know his voice and that they will not follow the voice of a stranger. If sons are truly hearing God and believe that they are sent to serve their father then the father's voice will be one to which they will respond. When true sons are corrected they respond peaceably. They can be taught and they are naturally and spiritually inclined to seek out the father's wisdom on matters of faith and life.

4) True sons are fruitful and faithful

As a result of faithfulness to the father and Christ, the son should be experiencing tangible and positive changes in his life (e.g. marriage, children, financial increase, favor with God and man, etc.). This isn't to say that faithful sons do not see trials and hard times but there should be a balance in which the son should be seeing the manifested blessings of the Lord in his life. Whether it is the fruit of the Spirit, gifts of the Spirit, or natural manifestations of favor, the son should be showing signs of reward because he has diligently sought the Lord by serving his spiritual father.

Naturally, true sons are faithful over the areas that they are assigned. They can be trusted with sensitive information such as when they see the human faults and failures of the father. When the father calls, sons show up consistently on time, ready, without excuse, and will communicate problems and setbacks. They will also grow personally in knowledge of the Word of God and in revelation.

5) True sons handle trials and persecution with faith and not flesh

The Bible guarantees that we will see trials and tests in our lives. However, those who are true sons are spirit-filled believers who respond to hardships with faith and not their flesh. When personal problems arise, the son's prayer life is evident. In the midst of pressure and pain, the son's connection with Jesus Christ manifests proving that they are truly in tune with the Savior.

The Attributes of False Sons

1) False sons have an improper view of the spiritual father and offer false praise

A false son's view of a spiritual father is inherently selfish and ultimately retains a purpose of self-promotion. When a false son praises his father, it is with the intent to flatter and not encourage strength in Christ. A false son will also attempt to step out of order by trying to manipulate or even correct the father. Sons are not in place to correct fathers. Fathers correct sons. If sons feel that a father is wrong their ultimate job is to pray but the correction of a father comes from the Heavenly Father and whomever the father submits to as a son.

2) False sons lack an evident prayer life

False sons do not pray. Sonship, in part, is the role of an intercessor for a father. False sons refuse to pray for their father or for anyone else. They do not fast nor do they hear the voice of God for himself or his family. These areas of lack can manifest in a number of ways; the major of which are those of murmuring and complaining about the father, ministry, or life in general.

3) False sons have ungodly motives

The purpose behind a false son's actions are to gain position and power. Whether by manipulation and flattery or by deceit and false balances, sons who are not sent by God will seek to use their trusted positions to gain more influence for selfish endeavors. In addition, false sons will be heard promoting their connection with the spiritual father more than a connection with Jesus Christ. The fruit of true sonship includes with it a stronger foundation in Christ. The motives of a false son will prove the foundation to be fleshly connections, positions of power, and greed.

4) False sons are prideful

The key goals for any false son center on self, self-preservation, and self-promotion. As a result, they are easily ensnared in pride and will lift themselves up above others. This will be evident in their lack of sacrifice; whether in the areas of time, money, or service, false sons will not sacrifice themselves unless there is some kind of recognition or personal gain.

5) False sons do not respond to the father's voice

Unlike the true sheep that hear the voice of Jesus in John 10, false sons will refuse to recognize the father's voice. When a false son is corrected, he does not receive it nor will he change his ways. False sons are not teachable and are unwilling to bow to the will of the father. Essentially, they think they know everything and cannot be taught.

6) False sons place their personal agendas over and above Kingdom Purpose

The heart of a false son will be evident in what goals he chases. He will constantly chase plans that are of personal benefit more than fulfilling his Kingdom assignments which he may find overly inconvenient.

7) False sons are unfruitful and unfaithful

Due to a lacking connection to the father and to Jesus, the false son will not produce good fruit. Issues will manifest that are obviously untied to general faith testing coming from the Lord. There will be financial issues, marital issues, family disconnections, and an obvious lack of the favor and protection of God due to unfaithfulness. They also do not care about Kingdom assignments or the father's purpose. When the father calls, a false son will be inconsistent with responses along with being untimely or not even showing up, having bad attitudes, or generating excuses for poor work. False sonship will also manifest in the family and in home life. They will not treat their families with honor, tenderness, and the love of Jesus. The same will apply to others, they will show a lack of love and a lack in the fruit of the Spirit while making strides in showing the works of the flesh (Galatians 5).

8)   False sons are easily persuaded by the flesh

Just as Gehazi ran after Naaman for a financial opportunity through lies and deceit, false sons will do the same. They will easily drop their mantle and run after worldly opportunities that provide them with personal glorification, even at the cost of the Kingdom.

9)   False sons handle persecution through the flesh

When persecution arises for being a part of ministry, false sons will react via the flesh. Their responses will be filled with man's reasoning, philosophy, and worldly tolerance instead of the Word of God. They lack patience and their lack of a prayer life will be evident not just in their verbal responses but in their overall actions as a result of Christian persecution.

The differences in true and false sons in ways are subtle but over time can be glaring. With the power of the Holy Spirit and study of the Word of God, true sons will stand to be utilized for the glory of God and false sons can be led to pray to receive a true experience with Jesus Christ.

CHAPTER 7 – JESUS: THE BELOVED SON

The ultimate example of sonship is none other than our Lord and Savior Jesus Christ. Anyone who has read through any of the Gospel accounts will find many references to Jesus' submission and sonship. It starts with his words; he made many references to God as his Father (Matt. 7:21, Luke 10:21). Even the model prayer that he gave the disciples when they asked him to teach them how to pray started with "Our Father (Luke 11:2)." As powerful as he was while on earth he constantly showed that he was under the authority of the Father whom he referenced as the orchestrator of the reason he was on earth. This relationship was not one-sided, not only did Jesus claim the Creator as his Father but the Father claimed Jesus, visually and audibly, as His son. After Jesus' baptism performed by John, the Father claimed him as His son in whom He was well pleased (Luke 3:21-22). In addition, on the mountain of transfiguration, God told the disciples that Jesus is His son and that they should listen to him (Luke 9:35). Even down to his death on the cross, Jesus commended his spirit into his Father's hands (Luke 23:46); showing that no matter what he was facing, he always knew who he was and, even more so, who his Father was.

Perhaps the most amazing thing about Jesus' life in relation to sonship is just how seamlessly submissive he was while being so sure about what his Father wanted and being swift to fulfill His will. He so loved the Father and the people in the world, he volunteered himself as a willing sacrifice to take on the sins of each individual that has lived and will live on the earth. In our sonship to any father that the Lord has assigned to us we should house the same mindset; that of choosing our father's will above our own. There will be times in sonship when a person's heart will be tested. Most times this simply comes in the form of instructions that the son either doesn't want to do or consist of parts that are extremely inconvenient. This isn't to say, in our modern society, that a son is some kind of slave to a father, but when a son is sent to a father there should be some level of dependability on the obedience of the son. In the case of Jesus Christ, perhaps his biggest test of sonship came in the moments before his crucifixion in the Garden of Gethsemane. While understanding that his time had come to be put to death, he prayed to the Father asking that if it was possible, that this cup (this request) would pass from him. Yet, in the midst of such pain he found within himself a love and resolve for the Father and His creation that he said "Nevertheless thy will be done." Although we may not face life or death decisions on a daily basis while serving our fathers, the very same attitude of Christ towards their instructions will need to apply. Essentially, the question that needs to be asked is how will you as a son treat another man's vision, dream, or ministry? Will you treat it as your own understanding that the Lord Himself is doing a work or will you think that serving someone else is a waste of time?

Laying down one's life for the benefit of another is never easy. In the 21ˢᵗ century we are taught daily about how important our pursuits should be. Whether its education, money, or love, society's thoughts of laying down one's own goals to completely assist someone else achieve theirs is not the normal outlook of life. However, Christ's entire life and everything he ever did was with 2 focuses in mind – his Father and us.

Although we must live balanced lifestyles to ensure the care of ourselves, our families, and those to whom we are responsible, there is a beauty behind gaining the mind of Christ in which there is a great amount of our lives that is devoted to someone other than ourselves. That is part of sonship. A part of our lives is dedicated to the building of the Kingdom of God and we are submitted to a person who is called out by God to lead this building. Our part in supporting this vision as sons is both critical and needed for the success of the Lord's Kingdom. Whether you become a son through close ministry ties,

"When the big picture and true purpose behind our service is seen, there isn't any way that we could see sonship as cumbersome or inconvenient."

service in church, graphic design, musical ability, or whatever the Lord has given you as a gift; each member of the Body of Christ comes together to do their part in helping the Gospel to reach every creature on the planet. Our sacrifices to the Lord in serving a father isn't about us; honestly, it's not even about the father, it's about the Lord Himself getting the glory and His Word reaching all of His creation so they can be won back to a relationship with Him. When the big picture and true purpose behind our service is seen, there isn't any way that we could see sonship as cumbersome or inconvenient. It becomes about the Lord's Kingdom

and each son who can see this fact will succeed in every endeavor as they support their father's vision.

Jesus Christ is the ultimate example of sonship and he operated on a level that we could never hope to attain without the power of the Holy Spirit working in us. It is by the Spirit that we gain power, the fruit of the Spirit, and the ability to do everything we are called to do – even sonship. It is beyond imperative that sons know Christ for themselves. Anyone claiming to be a son without knowing Christ has missed the point and purpose of true sonship. Sonship is all about the Kingdom of God and we cannot be true sons without knowing The Son. Jesus has to be the foundation in all that a son does, including service to a father. Without Christ, claiming sonship to a father is no more than someone joining a fraternity; it becomes a social standing for mankind to pride in themselves for the connection. However, with the Holy Spirit's leading we can fulfill our callings knowing that the Lord is pleased and He will one day say "Well done my good and faithful servant."

A fter all of the spiritual and biblical definitions along with the general points of life application, what does sonship actually look like in the 21ˢᵗ century from ministerial perspective? In what ways and roles can sonship be applied and how do we know that we are walking in the roles God ordained? This chapter will discuss some of the practical sonship roles we all can participate in and the rewards of sonship.

Practical Sonship Roles

Are you ready to apply sonship to your daily life in ministry? There are a number of practical roles that anyone with a heart for the Lord can take on to roll up their sleeves and put their hands to the work of the Kingdom as they are led by the Holy Spirit and the spiritual father to whom they are assigned.

1) Submitted Senior Pastors

Being a Senior Pastor of a flock essentially makes you a father to your flock. However, does that mean you are not a son? That couldn't be furthest from the truth. Everyone needs tangible guidance and direction, even those who are already Pastors. No matter how long someone has been pastoring or how large of a church he runs there is always someone out there who is doing it bigger, better, or differently. With the strain that comes with the role of a Pastor there needs to be someone covering the shepherd who can minister to those needs. How stressful can the role of a Pastor be? Let's answer that by saying there is a website called www.pastorburnout.com. The fact that such a site exists should answer the question. According to the site [9]:

- 1,500 pastors leave their ministries each month due to burnout, conflict, or moral failure
- 50% feel unable to meet the needs of the job
- 80% have insufficient time with their spouse
- 80% believe that pastoral ministry affects their families negatively
- 90% work more than 50 hours a week
- 94% feel under pressure to have a perfect family

Not only should this information press congregations to truly pray for their Pastors and leaders but should amplify the needs for Pastors to operate further in sonship. Having a spiritual father that can minister on a level that meets the Pastor's needs can help in reducing such staggering statistics. In this case, fathers who were once sons should pray to the Father so they can be led to be sons once again, even in their roles as fathers.

2) Armor Bearers

Perhaps one of the best roles that anyone can take on who has the heart of a son is that of an armor bearer. These assigned vessels walk closely with a Pastor or leader to assist in meeting their ministerial needs so they can flow in the Word of God and the Spirit of the Lord with minimal distraction. As intercessors, they pray for their leader. As ushers, they serve their leader. As ministers, they rehearse the Word of Life to their leaders. Biblical examples such as Nehemiah, young David, and Joshua were all in the operation of an armor bearer to their leaders. The reason this practical role is so powerful in the area of sonship is that, beyond friends, family, and other leaders; armor bearers will see some of the intricate sides of their father and the behind-the-scenes views of how everything in ministry works. Selection to this role should be taken very seriously as armor bearers must make sure that they are housing the presence of Jesus Christ at all times so they do not distract or disturb all that the Lord is doing through their assigned leader.

3) Assistant Pastors

Assistant Pastors, arguably, may have a job that is just as hard, if not harder, than the Senior Pastor. Why? Because many Assistant Pastors do the work of the ministry, teach and preach wonderfully, lead groups, visit the sick, marry and counsel couples, and anything else that a Senior Pastor would do; just without the accolades. Many may agree with the statement that says 'it is easy to find people who want to be number 1 but a great deal harder to find good people who will be number 2.' So why is this role so good for sonship? Because if you are just as gifted in shepherding as a Senior Pastor but you are willing, by the leading of the Lord, to be the assistant then you are truly laying down your life for the better of the Kingdom. That takes a level of sonship that many in the 21st century do not have. The world and media say we all need to be running our own companies, leading the pack, and looking out for ourselves. Yet there are not many voices celebrating those who support those who are leading the pack. While the President is the talk of the nation, how many know what the Vice-President does as his job? But not many know just how much the ones in the spotlight depend on the ones in the background. Those who have the opportunity to serve the Lord and a father as an Assistant Pastor have a seriously difficult and challenging undertaking to support the support system that everyone else leans on. They run churches, pray for everyone, and take on loads of stress without their names in the

"Not many know just how much the ones in the spotlight depend on the ones in the background."

lights. Assistant Pastors are true sons as they operate in the Spirit of the Lord and are truly blessed as they continue to carry, communicate, and enact the visions of the father of the house to which they are assigned.

4) Elders, Deacons, and Ministry Leaders

From Youth Pastors to Parking Lot attendants along with Ministers and Lay Leaders; all of whom operate as sons of the Lord and sons of the father of their house. Ushers, Cooks, Janitors, and Children's Church workers – All of whom are the people that make things happen and keep the Kingdom running. Each of them are sons of the father as they are the hands that make the visions come to pass in real life. Without people through whom the work of the ministry operates, the father is just speaking to the air. Praise the Lord for the workers and leaders, many of them unsung heroes, who work tirelessly to make sure that the Gospel reaches the ears of those who need to know that Jesus loves them.

5) Church Members

Those who believe in Jesus Christ and grow to be daily disciples are the sheep that represent the Lord on their jobs, at home, and wherever they go. Even if they don't work in church, they are sons who support the vision of the father financially and take the Gospel to their corner of the world where a church worker may never go. Every disciple has a practical role in sonship, spread the Gospel and let your light shine so that the Lord can be glorified by your work and your testimony.

Rewards of Sonship

As we take on our roles in sonship and practically work to bring about glory to the Lord, what are the rewards we can expect? Although we know that we are sons because we just love the Lord, there are rewards that come for diligent and faithful service that only our God can offer.

1) An Inheritance as Heirs and Joint Heirs

As sons and believers, we are engrafted into the spiritual lineage of Abraham and we are also joint-heirs with Jesus Christ. With this, the same promises that we see given by God to others apply to us. When we see in Deuteronomy 28 the blessings that come with obedience we know that they will manifest in our lives as sons. As you read Revelation and find that we are promised to ascend with Christ and enjoy New Jerusalem in the presence of God, you know that your sonship is not in vain. Review the promises of God in His Word, apply them your life, and know that you have inherited all of these blessings because you honor Him by serving Him.

2) Passing of the Anointing and the Blessing

Just as with the transfer of mantles from Elijah to Elisha, we as faithful sons will see transfers coming from our fathers to our lives. When you serve a father, the anointing on his life can pass down to sons along with the blessings that empowers us to do great things in the earth realm. This is why it is important to choose a father wisely. Ask yourself what anointing and what blessing are you looking to receive. If the father you have chosen houses those blessings then faithful sonship can result in the transfer of the blessing when the time comes. Just as Isaac transferred the Abrahamic blessing to Jacob the same would apply to a spiritual father to a son.

3) True Power

Simon the Sorcerer in the book of Acts wanted to pay for the power of the Holy Spirit but he didn't realize that the power came from a relationship with Christ. The same applies to the power that a father houses for his ministry. Whatever grace that the Lord has given the father is manifested by the power of God through a relationship with God. Yet, in the same vein, much power that men and women of God have is activated by the laying on of hands just as Paul mentioned he did to Timothy. A son's true power is unlocked by someone who can see it and has the Godly authority to unlock it. Without a father who covers a son, a person can only operate a portion of his potential. True sonship that builds a relationship with the father leads to the unlocking of true power.

4) Seals of Approval

When Nehemiah went off to go rebuild the walls of Jerusalem, his years of sonship and favor with his King won him seals of approval in the form of resources, materials, and letters that backed his mission. When we, as true sons, serve to the best of our ability in a consistent manner over time; when the time comes where favor is needed of the father, seals of approval are granted. When you go off to start your own ministry or business the father's blessing will go with you and any weight that the father's name carries (in the natural or spiritual) goes with you as well. Faithfulness to fathers lead to seals of approval that will support all that you do.

5) Trust

A reward that cannot be assigned a value is that of trust. When you can be trusted with money, ministry, and lives there isn't much that you won't be allowed to do as a son. When a father's heart can rest in the fact that he can trust his son, he will grant favor and access that would not apply to others. Trust is an invaluable reward that opens doors to all that the Lord has to offer.

6) Pedigree

One of the more powerful rewards of sonship is that of pedigree. You have a name that is attached to great names from which you can build rapport and reputation. Elisha was spoken of as one who poured water on the hands of Elijah. That statement alone puts Elisha on a level of respect and honor that would not have come from just his name alone. It showed that he learned and was trained by the best in his field. There is also someone to reference in his history that speaks volumes about his power, his character, and his ability. The same applies to 21st century sonship. When you serve faithfully, you gain a reputation; and with that reputation comes a connection to your father's name. With that name you gain a historical pedigree that proves who you are, what you know, and where you came from.

7) Passing the Torch

Moses passed the leadership torch to Joshua when the Lord instructed him to do so. The ultimate reward of sonship, whether or not you're the one chosen, is to be considered as one who could be trusted to carry on the mission of your father. In the 21st century we call this concept succession planning. In other words, who will take over when the leader's time has come to an end? Today, many Pastors and leaders may retire but they spent years prior to the decision training up a group from the younger generation as possible replacements. When the Lord speaks, they choose who will be next to carry on the mission. To even be considered as one who could possibly be a Joshua to a current Moses is an honor itself. This honor only comes to those who are faithful sons to a father who is ready to pass the torch.

Practical sonship is the application of the Art of Sonship in roles that exercise the principles found in the scriptures. With these applications come rewards that prove and validate the son's value, service, and calling. One day the son who serves a father may become a father raising sons.

Thishis final chapter will shortly emphasize the point that introduced the entire book – Good sons become great fathers. Biblically we can see the fruit of great sons such as Joshua, Elisha, Samuel, Timothy, and Titus who grew to become great fathers of the faith. Joshua led the Children of Israel to the Promised Land; Elisha performed twice the amount of miracles than that of his predecessor Elijah; Samuel grew to anoint Kings, judge Israel, and start the prophetic movement; Timothy became the Bishop overseeing the church at Ephesus; and Titus became the Bishop overseeing the church at Crete. But studying and analyzing biblical history is only part of the process towards sonship. Practical application through roles and service must be done to prove one's sonship and reap the rewards. But when all is said and done – Where does that leave you?

"Without sons, everything will eventually cease to exist ... without fathers, the sons won't know what to do or where to go."

Yes you, reading this book – Where does all of this information, revelation, and application leave you? Are you operating as a son? Are you working in your full purpose for the Lord who created you? Take the time to pray about your assignment. Whether you've been in ministry for decades or you just received Christ last week, sonship applies to us all. If you know who your spiritual father should be or if you are still learning about your Heavenly Father, sonship is still yours to claim. Why is sonship so important? It goes back to the points shared in the very beginning of this book – Without sons, everything will eventually cease to exist. Yet we can add this point: without fathers, the sons won't know what to do or where to go.

If you are a good son, may the Lord bless you to eventually become a great father. This does not mean you need to Pastor or even be a minister. But what it means is that you would grow to be one who is willing not only to serve but to guide and lead others to serve. Whatever your gift, whatever your ministry; meditate on how your sonship can grow into fatherhood. Fathers produce after their own kind. They raise sons and mold them to be great men and fathers in the natural realm. Spiritually, apply your sonship, grow to be a father, and teach others that come behind you how to grow in the Lord and give themselves back to Him as sons.

For [even the whole] creation (all nature) waits expectantly and longs earnestly for God's sons to be made known [waits for the revealing, the disclosing of their sonship].

Romans 8:19 (AMP)

CHAPTER 10 – BONUS POINTS TO CONSIDER

The book was completed and I looked over what I wrote excited about this concept of sonship and elated to prepare it for the world to see. But as with any Holy-Spirit-led endeavor, I found that when I was done writing, God was not done speaking. The first 9 chapters you just finished reading were written out of much planning, prayer, and organization. When the book was done, I couldn't help but know that there was more to bring forth. So, like a good son, I waited for the Father to speak. I let this book sit on the shelf for about 6 to 8 months nearly fearing that I would be commanded to erase it all and start from scratch, but I let it sit patiently waiting on the Father to teach me more.

Since the writing, my church had a conference in which one of the speakers was assigned to speak on . . . you guessed it, SONSHIP. The timing was impeccable (since God orchestrated it), I had just finished the book and the Lord had me lay it down for a moment. So I knew that there was more that I needed to hear and more I needed to learn. After the conference, some of my ministry brothers and sisters spoke on the topic of sonship – some with understanding and some with many questions still in their minds. I knew then why the Lord was sending this book out. Sonship, though not a foreign concept, is still misunderstood, still mysterious, and, in some cases, still mishandled. Over a few more months of prayer and meditation came more points that I believe the Lord would have me to share as we continue to gain further understanding of Sonship.

Sonship Validates Fatherhood

The 9 chapters that made up this book mainly spoke from the perspective of the son understanding his role in the father-son relationship. While I will reserve elaboration on spiritual fatherhood for a future work (if the Lord wills), I can say simply that sonship validates fatherhood. In 2 Corinthians 3, we'll find Paul saying to the Corinthian church that they are his letters (epistles) that prove his Apostleship. In other words, the fact that they are Believers growing in the faith and living for Christ

A father's true validation in the role of a father comes only through the success of his sons.

proves that his role as a father has been effective. When a father has ministerial sons that are successfully continuing the work of the ministry, that father's ministry is validated and commended by the son's success. While the father could celebrate many accolades and accomplishments that he has performed personally, his true validation, as a father, comes only through the success of his sons. Just as a father in the natural world cannot call himself a father without having children, the same applies in the spiritual – A spiritual father cannot be recognized as one if spiritual sons have not risen up to call him father. That should be a challenge to all who claim to be sons. Your performance and success (or lack thereof) is a reflection of your father. While he cannot be

blamed for individual decisions, he will be referenced when questions arise like 'where were you trained?' As a son, validating the fatherhood of a father is more than just some information, it grows quickly to be a serious responsibility.

Violations In Sonship

Just as sons can validate fathers – They can also violate fathers. In a previous chapter, the discussion of the birthright and how it applied in historical sonship was discussed. In your study time, take a look at the story of Reuben, the son of Jacob. Reuben was the first born to Jacob and, under normal circumstances, was the one with the birthright and all of the benefits of being the firstborn son. In Genesis 35:22, Reuben made a sonship violation by laying with his father's concubine Bilhah. When you see the word violation in the dictionary, there will be multiple definitions that relate to two main areas – The law and holy articles. When we as citizens of our country violate our country's laws, we are forced to pay fines or, in major cases, we are incarcerated. When holy articles, in Biblical history, were desecrated in some way, there were spiritual repercussions (Ref. Uzzah touching the Ark of God – 2 Sam. 6:7). So, Reuben, by laying with his father's concubine, not only violated a spiritual law but, in the process, would forego his sonship rights as a punishment.

1 Chronicles 5:1-2 says: *Now the sons of Reuben the firstborn of Israel, (for he was the firstborn;* **but, forasmuch as he defiled his father's bed, his birthright was given unto the sons of Joseph the son of Israel:**

*and the genealogy is **not to be reckoned after the birthright**. For Judah prevailed above his brethren, and of him came the chief ruler; **but the birthright was Joseph's:**). (Emphasis Added)*

Note that because Reuben violated his father's bed, he lost his sonship rights – He lost his birthright. Not only that, but it was given to Joseph. What does this mean? The birthright, as discussed earlier, gave the firstborn son a double portion of an inheritance and authority over the family upon the father's death. Essentially, Reuben lost all of his inheritance and his authority due to his sonship violation. Beyond the spiritual implications and his blessings, his violation cost him his relationship with his father. In his final words to all of his sons, Jacob said to Reuben *"Reuben, thou art my firstborn, my might, and the beginning of my strength, the excellency of dignity, and the excellency of power: **Unstable as water, thou shalt not excel; because thou wentest up to thy father's bed; then defiledst thou it: he went up to my couch.**" (Genesis 49:3-4, Emphasis Added).* Reuben lost it all and, most importantly, he lost his connection to his father.

While, in our day and age, we may judge Reuben and say over and over again what we wouldn't do to our fathers and how we would never violate them, I would argue that we, as sons, risk violations more than we think. When we backbite or gossip about our fathers, we're violating trust. When we disobey orders, we're violating honor. When we think of ourselves as higher than them, we violate order and submission. When we indulge in the works of the flesh as outlined in Galatians 5, we violate our covenants. Take care, as you serve, not to violate your father. You cannot afford to lose your connection, your inheritance, or your blessings as you attempt to go forth in all that God has for you.

Sons and the Father's Legacy

Sons must know that they are their father's legacy. All that sons do are, ultimately, a reflection of their father. Sons are more than just those who get to carry the Man of God's Bible or those who get to stand beside him during high holy times; they are investments into a legacy that the father is seeking to leave behind. Everyone who considers himself or herself a son or daughter must realize that a responsibility is being taken on. That responsibility is to help build and preserve the legacy of your father. When everyone sees you and celebrates, that's a celebration of your father's legacy. When they frown or curse you, that is a negative reflection of your father's legacy. Sons and daughters, we have a great mission that is ahead of us. As we represent Jesus Christ in all that we do we also carry the representation of our fathers as well. I pray, that as you go forth in sonship and gain your true inheritance from your father that you would arise to become all that God has made you to be to represent Heaven well and also do your part to build the legacy of the one who trained you and sent you forth.

REFERENCES

[1] Thayer & Smith. (n.d.). Greek Lexicon entry for Apokalupto. *The KJV New Testament Greek Lexicon.* Retrieved from http://www.biblestudytools.com/lexicons/greek/kjv/apokalupto.html

[2] Apprenticeship. (n.d.) Retrieved from http://en.wikipedia.org/wiki/Apprenticeship

[3] Pitts, J. (2014). *Ministering to Millennials: The Challenges of Reaching Generation Why.* Greater Works Publishing.

[4] Brown, Driver, Briggs, & Gesenius. (n.d.) Hebrew Lexicon entry for Mashach. *The NAS Old Testament Hebrew Lexicon.* Retrieved from http://www.biblestudytools.com/lexicons/hebrew/nas/mashach.html

[5] Smith, Dr. W. (1901). Entry for Anointing. *Smith's Bible Dictionary.* Retrieved from http://www.biblestudytools.com/dictionaries/smiths-bible-dictionary/anointing.html

[6] Easton, M. (1897). Entry for Birthright. *Easton's Bible Dictionary.* Retrieved from http://www.biblestudytools.com/dictionary/birthright/

[7] Smith, Dr. W. (1901). Entry for Birthright. *Smith's Bible Dictionary.* Retrieved from http://www.biblestudytools.com/dictionary/birthright/

[8] Orr, J. (1915). Entry for BIRTHRIGHT. *International Standard Bible Encyclopedia.* Retrieved from http://www.biblestudytools.com/dictionary/birthright/

[9] Sherman, D. (2010). Pastor Burnout Statistics. Retrieved from http://www.pastorburnout.com/pastor-burnout-statistics.html

ABOUT THE AUTHOR

Jonathan G. Pitts, the Kingdom Empowerment Catalyst, is a cutting-edge visionary who seeks to lead an end-time generation to embrace their divine purposes. As an Entrepreneur, Author, Speaker, and Teacher he is a thought-provoking developer of the mind who has the ultimate purpose of drawing people nearer to God and a greater understanding of Kingdom Principles. His gift as a Kingdom Builder provides life-giving blueprints from which the Body of Christ can emerge victorious in all areas of ministry.

Jonathan, is the Founder of Ignite Ministries through which he and his wife Juarkena minister and build God's people and develop them to reach their goals in ministry, marriage, parenthood, business, and more. He is also the Founder and CEO of Greater Works Enterprises, LLC., a business conglomerate offering services specializing in publishing, graphic design, and small business consulting. In addition, he is the Founder of The Greater Works Foundation, a non-profit organization that provides outreach to underprivileged, under-served, and underrepresented youth and communities by promoting financial literacy, educational enrichment, leadership skills, mentoring, and global service initiatives that will cultivate the next generation of responsible leaders thereby creating empowered citizens and communities.

Jonathan has appeared on the Trinity Broadcasting Network and is a sought-after ministry strategist providing wisdom and insight in a variety of areas. He is the author of several books and studies including:

- Ministering to Millennials: The Challenges of Reaching Generation "Why"
- 21st Century Sonship: Restoring the Art of Apprenticeship
- The Church Leader's Guide to Millennial Engagement
- Heaven's Sound: Call to the Nations
- And More!

He is the proud husband of Juarkena Pitts and the honored father of 3 wonderful children.

www.ingramcontent.com/pod-product-compliance
Lightning Source LLC
Chambersburg PA
CBHW031605040426
42452CB00006B/416